CW01335820

Blaydon

in old picture postcards

included: Winlaton

by
N.G. Rippeth

European Library – Zaltbommel/Netherlands

GB   ISBN 90 288 4833 9 / CIP

© 1989 European Library – Zaltbommel/Netherlands

INTRODUCTION

The area covered by this book formed the southern and eastern Townships of the ancient parish of Ryton. Both townships, Stella and Winlaton, probably date back to Saxon times or earlier and were mentioned in the Bolden Buke, a twelfth century tax survey carried out for Hugh Pudsey, Prince Bishop of Durham.

The survey followed the end of the civil war between King Stephen and Empress Matilda, during which King David of Scotland annexed Northumberland north of the Tyne. It is thought probable that David fortified Ryton to secure a river crossing, as both Prudhoe and Newcastle were held by Stephen's lords. The chaos that followed the Scottish withdrawal probably explains how Stella, gifted earlier to the nuns of Newcastle in perpetuity, was held by the son of Thomas the moneyer, the Bishop's minter, when the Bolden Buke was compiled.

The Stella area contains archaeological evidence of much earlier occupation. Burial kists have been found which date back to the new stone age. The contents of these kists show evidence that these earliest inhabitants of the Blaydon area believed in an afterlife. The flint tools that have been unearthed from time to time, together with the discovery of a dugout canoe near the Tyne, suggest that the new stone age society in the area had wide trading links as well as a theology. The Romans came, stayed a few centuries, and withdrew leaving little in the immediate area to remind us they had been. Then came the Saxons who settled in both the Tyne and Derwent valleys. Winlaton Mill is the site of one of many local Saxon settlements. It was threatened and probably burned by Viking raiders.

When the Normans conquered England they regarded Bernicia, or English Northumbria, as a frontier buffer state, where it was impossible to get white bread, and where the inhabitants were wild. The roasting alive of King William's nominee for the earldom of Northumberland by a Saxon rival in Newburn Church, and the murder of William's bishop in the church door at Gateshead, prompted dire retribution. The conquerer moved swiftly and 'harried' the North. Winlaton Mill was one of hundreds of villages to be burned. The inhabitants who were not killed either died of starvation or were taken by the Scots as slaves. For nearly a century the land lay wasted, the Domesday survey did not bother to record its existence.

By the middle of the twelfth century small settlements were re-established, at river crossings such as that at Winlaton Mill and at the confluence of the Tyne and Blaydon Burn at Blaydon. By the time of the Bolden survey these were little more than farm hamlets. This typical medieval pattern of land use, agricultural hamlets, was supplemented within two centuries by the development of organized coalmining by the bishop's agents. The early mines were under the control of the bishop's head forester. This position had the title of 'Viewer'. This name was to pass into the vocabulary of the coalmining industry. By the year 1367, coal mined on the hill that was to become Winlaton town, was being shipped from Blaydon to Windsor where it was burned with limestone to produce the lime needed for the morter used to build the castle. Coalmining and the townships of Blaydon and Winlaton developed together over the next 200 years. Winlaton became the largest producer of coal, while Blaydon grew as the home of the keelmen. The keelmen ferried the coal in shallow draught boats downriver to seagoing colliers. By the closing years of 'Good Queen Bess' Blaydon's role as a shipping point was augmented when it became the end of the 'lead road' from Allendale. As the mining of lead developed on the moors around Allendale the industry developed at Blaydon where a leadworks was built.

Meanwhile the ready supply of coal at Winlaton attracted Ambrose Crowley to establish Ironworks both at Winlaton, and, attracted by the potential for water driven machines, at Winlaton Mill. The Crowley Company built squares of blacksmith's workshops and ran the communities using a social system developed on Quaker ideals. The medical, educational, spiritual and economic welfare of the workers was catered for, literally, from the cradle to the grave. The Allendale leadmine owners adopted a similar system for their miners.

The end of the Napoleonic wars caused a slump in trade and the withdrawal of the Crowley Co. from Winlaton. However, the development of Blaydon as a railway town brought a period of relative prosperity, while the increase in demand for 'steamcoal' gave the local collieries a new lease of life. We pick up the story of Blaydon and Winlaton through the camera's eye as this period of Peace and Plenty was coming to a close.

I have been assisted in the compilation of the postcards and photographs by:
Gateshead M.B.C. Local Studies Section, Central Library;
Bill Pears of Rowlands Gill;
George Friars of Ryton;
Trevor Ashworth of Winlaton;
John Carrick and Peter Waugh of Crawcrook.

I have drawn on the following histories:
Bourne: *History of Ryton* (1896);
Maughan: *History of Blaydon* (1955-7);
Winlaton L.H.Soc: *History of Blaydon* (1974).

Ryton, 1989

N.G. Rippeth

1. *Stella Colliery, Addison, about 1920.* This colliery was named after the first managing director of the Stella Coal Co. The colliery, together with the associated offices at Low Hedgefield, was the headquarters of the company in the years before nationalisation. This card shows the pithead from the road up to Stella. The buildings that are visible in the foreground include the winding gear for the cage and part of the roof of the screening sheds. Addison Colliery had both a shaft and a drift. The drift ran West and entered the ground to the North and West of the end of Low Row. Coal was led to the bottom of the shaft on narrow gauge railways. The coal was carried in small iron wagons called tubs, these were hauled by sturdy pit ponies called 'Galloways'. These ponies were the descendants of the pack ponies used for centuries to carry lead ore to Blaydon. In the distance can be seen the Tyne and, on the other bank, Newburn Iron Works chimneys.

2. *Addison Colliery; last shift up before the general strike 1926*. This photograph was taken by Walter Tate of Stella. These men and boys, passing the pit props in the colliery yard, were putters and drivers. The putters were responsible for taking the coal from the hewers at the coal face and loading it into the tubs. The drivers then led the pit ponies that pulled the tubs to the shaft. The tubs were then raised to the surface in the cage, a 'lift' which travelled up and down the shaft, guided by steel rails that ran the length of the shaft. Notice the two types of lamps carried. The open lamps burned acetylene gas, produced in the lamp by dripping water onto calcium carbide. These lamps could only be used in 'safe' areas, free of gas. The other lamps are safety lamps. These are called 'Geordie' lamps, after George Stephenson, who first designed them. Elsewhere they are known as 'Davy' lamps, as Sir Humphrey Davy independently came up with the design in London, six months after Stephenson.

3. *Blaydon Races about 1912.* Racing began in Blaydon in the early 1800s. The first site for the course was where the railway station stands today. The Races ceased in 1835 when the railway opened, and were not revived until 1861, when they were held on an island in the Tyne, just north of the station. The song which immortilised the races was written in 1862, and relates the adventures of a party from Newcastle, and the rainy weather on race day. The races were transferred to this, their final site, on Stella Haughs in 1887. Stella South Power Station now covers the site. Racing ceased after the 1916 meeting, when a riot broke out following the disqualification of the favourite, after the last race. The wooded hill to the left in the picture was the site of the English fortifications at the battle of Newburn in 1640. A small English force attempted, unsuccessfully, to stop the Scottish Army crossing the Tyne. The houses in the background stood near Newburn bridge and were known locally as 'Klondyke'.

4. *Moving house about 1920*. This photo was taken near the railway crossing at Stella. The crossing led to Harrison's stables and the racecourse. The cart carries the contents of a typical pit cottage, with the mangle and wooden poss tub visible at the front of the load. The cart is moving down the main road, past Tempest Street and Cromwell Street towards Blaydon. Many pit widows and, after 1914, war widows, brought up their families by taking in washing. Whilst the 'big houses' of the Simpson, Cowen, Priestley, or Clavering families had their own laundries and staff, most of the tradespeople and professionals living in the smart new terraces of the area depended on the washerwomen.

5. *Stella Hall: 1900*. Stella Hall occupied the site of an ancient Nunnery. The Nuns of Newcastle were given Stella by a Bishop of Durham in 1149. This card shows the hall as it was in Jos. Cowen Jnr.'s time. The hall was originally built during the 16th century by the Tempest family. It was enlarged in the 18th century by Payne, the architect of Axwell hall. John Dobson made further alterations in 1840. Jos. Cowen Snr. started his career as an apprentice chainmaker in 'Crowley's crew'. When Crowley left Winlaton, Cowen formed the Blacksmiths' Friendly Society in 1826. In 1828 he started making bricks at Blaydon Burn, by 1850 he was able to buy Stella Hall, and was elected M.P. for Newcastle in 1865. He built the Blaydon Gas Works and helped found the Blaydon Co-operative Society. He died in 1873. Jos. Cowen Jnr. took over his fathers's seat in the Commons in 1874. Both father and son were radicals, corresponding with patriots in Hungary and Poland by sealing messages into bricks.

6. *Wounded soldiers 'welcome home' at Stella Hall 1918.* When Jos. Cowen jnr. died in 1900, his daughter Jane lived on in the hall. Jane was noted throughout the area for her works of charity and her continuation in practical ways of the family's concern for the people. Here she is entertaining war wounded of the Blaydon district at Stella Hall. The Great War was to see the realisation of the family vision of democratic nation states replacing the autocratic empires of Europe. The cost in human suffering was particularly acute locally, as the miners of Durham flocked to the colours, and raised more battalions than any other county. Many never returned, or, like the veterans in the photo, came back wounded, gassed or shell-shocked.

7. *Stella House.* This house stands near the bottom of the 'lead road', on Summerhill Bank. It was built early in the 18th century as the home of the Silvertop family. They were Roman-Catholic coal owners, who gave refuge to priests fleeing the French Revolution. It is said that a passage existed down which catholic fugitives escaped the mob after the Jacobite risings. Blaydon keelmen nicknamed the house the 'rising Sun' because of its position. In the 19th century it became the residence of T.Y.Hall, the mining engineer who invented the 'cage'. The first cage was installed in the shaft of nearby Woodside Pit. Before the cage, coal and men had to travel up the shaft in a large basket called a corve.

8. *Cowens Crossing: Blaydon about 1920.* This bridge carried what was, for centuries, the only road between Gateshead and Hexham. It bridges Blaydon Burn just south of its confluence with the River Tyne. The coal trucks on the loading hoppers are at the end of the line from the Mary and Bessie drift mines at Blaydon Burn village about a mile upstream. Coal was transferred from here to carts for local use or onto the Newcastle to Carlisle railway. Coal was also offloaded onto keels which sailed up the burn. Keelmen provided the bulk of the population of Blaydon before the railway came. The building in the right background was built by the Crowley Co. as a warehouse in the 18th century.

9. *Old Blaydon; from Cowens buildings.* A postcard taken about 1900. These tenements date back to early in the 19th century. They were built to house workers in the new heavy industries that sprang up around the railway. They were built just to the west of the sight of the old lead works. Silver extracted from Allendale lead at Blaydon was used in the coins of George II. The flotation process for extracting the silver from the lead ore was developed here by Parkes. The very tall signal post is to enable drivers to see the semaphore board clearly against the sky. The lattice work pole and pointed ferrel are characteristic of the North Eastern Railway Co.

10. *Bridge Street Blaydon about 1900.* This housing, dating back to the late 18th century, was stone built and had both stone and pantiles as roofing. It was originally occupied by keelmen, and would have been the centre of the old town in the days when the lead works were operating. Most of the houses on Bridge Street were demolished when the straight and level new road and bridge were built over Blaydon Burn.

11. *Dr. Brown's surgery, Blaydon, about 1900.* Dr. Richard Brown M.B. surgeon, supplied the medical needs of the community at Blaydon around the turn of the century. His qualifications, as listed in Kelly's Directory for 1895, reflect the days before surgeons were given equal status with physicians. His house is in sharp contrast with the dwellings on the two earlier cards, reflecting the vast divide between the housing conditions of the professional classes and the hovels endured by the working classes of the time. Notice the horse-drawn trap in the courtyard and the family pet at the door. In the days before the National Health Service most workers paid a few pence into a mutual insurance scheme every week, to pay the doctor's bills in times of serious illness. The local chemist, Robt. Cubey at 6 Church Street, was called upon to supply the needs of less serious complaints with a range of patent medicines nearer the range of the worker's pockets.

12. *Looking down Tyne Street, Blaydon about 1900.* This postcard shows the shops and houses side of the street. The other side consisted of a sawmill, a railway wagon factory, the station and the goods yard. The architectural variety in the street reflects the mix of housing, shops, banks and hotels that made up the street. In 1895 the street boasted three butchers, three confectioners, two shoemakers, a bank, a tailors shop, a building society and a fishmongers. Amongst the private residents were several tradesmen including joiners, painters and an Inspector of Nuisances! Notice the white edging on the steps and the all white threshold stones by the front door to the left of Rowland's sweetshop. Local housewives took a pride in their front steps, woe betide any man of child that marked the white edge! The horse is pulling a cart of the type used by Walter Willson and the Co-op. to deliver groceries.

13. *Blaydon Station about 1900.* The railway came to Blaydon on 9th March 1835, when the first passengers were carried on the section of line from Blaydon to Hexham, the first part of the Newcastle to Carlisle Railway to be opened. At the time there was less than 300 miles of track anywhere in the world. The card shows the older buildings and uncovered footbridge of the station, which was later rebuilt and given a glass roof. The glass was blown out during an air-raid in 1942. The opening of the railway gave working people the chance to take trips to Ryton Willows or Haydon Spa on their day off, which was Sunday. This prompted one local clergyman to publish a pamphlet against these excursions entitled 'Day Trips To Hell For 7/6'. Another vicar, who liked the railway, paid for the installation of a set of small organ pipes on a N & C loco, so that 'edifying hymn tunes' could by played on the Sabbath.

14. *Blaydon, station platform about 1900.* The young man on the right is wearing a sailor suit. This was when Britannia really ruled the waves, and all boys would could had sailor suits. The colourful display of adverts and the fancy cast iron were also typical of the time. A wooden bridge was built to carry the railway across the Tyne from Blaydon in 1838. This saved passengers having to complete the journey to Newcastle by ferryboat. By 1860 the bridge was reported to be in poor repair. An inspector was sent from the board of trade who ran a loco from Blaydon over the bridge, where-upon cinders from the firebox fell on the bridge and burned it down. It was replaced with another wooden bridge until 1868, when the present iron bridge was built.

15. *Tyne Street late 1890's.* This card showing the lower end of the street, just before the rail crossing, shows the ends of Cuthbert and Robinson Streets. The large gas lamp was one of the originals, put up in 1853. Joseph Cowen supplied the gas for Blaydon from the gasworks he had built to supply lighting for the brickworks. Funds to cover the cost of 'lighting up' Blaydon were raised by a public rate fixed at a public meeting in the Mechanics Hall. The meeting was held on 6th December 1853 and chaired by Dr. Brown. The lady holding the child to the window of the sweetshop is wearing a white apron or pinafore. This style was worn by ladies of all classes from the Queen to the scullery maid. Notice the crowd waiting for the 'pub' to open.

Blaydon. 3513

16. *Tyne Street and Church Street, Blaydon about 1920.* The building at the junction of the two streets contained a pub as well as the corner shop. The pub contained the 'Long bar', which stretched across from the entrance in Tyne Street to the door on Church Street. The card's central feature is the signal gantry used to control the junction between the Scotswood & Dunston lines as well as the goods siding. The 'new' gas lamps while less substantial than the originals, are still quite heavily ornamented. The cart is a brewer's dray, delivering some of the large load of barrels it carries to the pub. The almost total lack of traffic and the manner with which the street is used as a footpath is a reminder of the lack of private transport for most of the people of the time.

17. *Church Street about 1890.* This postcard shows Church Street before the building of the Empire Electric Theatre. In the distance can be seen the old whitewashed houses of Wesley Square. Outside the entrance to Northumberland House are five of the original gas lamps dating back to 1853. Tyne Street is unmetalled with gutters down each side, one gutter runs across Church Street. The only traffic on Tyne Street are farm carts, a reminder that Blaydon, in spite of its factories, was surrounded by the fields that had provided its staple industry for over a thousand years.

18. *Foot of Church Street, 'The Empire' about 1915.* This card shows both a motor car and a cart on the road to the left, the surface of the road has been tarmacadamed and the cinema has arrived in Blaydon! The classical, well-decorated façade of the Empire boasted, 'Drama', 'Music' and 'Travel'. It was built as an Electric Theatre very similar in design to a Music Hall, with circle, stalls and pit. The 'music' came from a piano in the pit under the screen and accompanied the silent films of the time. Older residents may recall the epics and Chaplin comedies. Others will no doubt remember the Saturday afternoon childrens Matinees. The young patrons were given a programme of cartoon, serial and main feature. On several occasions in the 1940's and 1950's, when the main feature failed to arrive the standby 'Charge at Feather River' was screened. This invariably provoked a near riot and an early end to the matinee. The Empire closed its doors before 'bingo' and was replaced with a branch of Woolworths.

19. *Church Street, Blaydon about 1900.* This card shows the main shopping street in Blaydon in its prime. On the right is the Blaydon Co-operative Society, and on the left is Walter Willson at the corner with Wesley Square. The earth road is rutted by the metal tyres of various carts and the footsteps of the pedestrians. The lady in the centre has a full length skirt, of typical Edwardian fashion, trailing in the dirt. The men all wear flat caps. A man's station in life was signified by his headgear, workers wore caps, foremen and managers wore bowlers also known locally as 'Duts', and mine and factory owners (the 'Toffs') wore top hats. However, the toffs wore a variation of the workers cap when out shooting or playing golf. None of the buildings were more than seventy years old when this photograph was taken, as the town centre developed when the railway arrived. The church after which the street was named, is St. Cuthberts, and predates the larger buildings shown here. Today only the church remains.

20. *Wesley Place, Blaydon about 1928.* This card shows the left window of Walter Willson, several smaller shops, and across the road, Lloyds Bank. In the background is the Railway Station, with the poster board, displaying the LNER logo. Although the Newcastle to Carlisle line was totally LNER, the arrangement that had been set up between the North Eastern and North British Railways involving shared use of lines gave the LMS the right to run a train a day through Blaydon to Newcastle. Wesley Place is a reminder of the impact the Wesley brothers had locally, especially in the mining villages. Blaydon appears on an early Wesleyan Preaching Plan (dated 1835), and the old buildings that were replaced when the square was built included a Wesleyan Chapel, opened in 1856.

21. *Wesley Place; Blaydon 1930s.* This card taken in the early thirties, shows Wesley Place at the height of the depression. The news boards outside Todd's papershop tell of coal company mergers, as the demand for coal dropped. Blaydon, a town built around coal, the factories that burned it and the railway that used and carried it, suffered more than most places. The male unemployment rate was above 70% for most of the thirties. It is doubtful if the men standing outside the Red Lion felt like joining Gracie Fields at the Empire as she exhorted them to 'Sing as we go'. This square, which for decades had echoed to the Salvation Army Band telling the patrons of the Red Lion to 'Stand up for Jesus' or 'Cling to the old rugged cross' was used by Mosley's Blackshirts attempting to recruit the unemployed into the British Fascist Movement.

22. *The Blaydon Co-operative Society.* This fine emporium, constructed with typical late Victorian panache, the upper windows reflecting the vogue for ancient Egyptian styling, was the headquarters of the Blaydon Industrial & Providential Society. This society was formed in 1858, with encouragement from Jos.Cowens. It was the second society to be founded in the country. The 'Co-op' movement began to enable the working people to supply themselves with the necessities of life without a 'middleman' raking off a profit. Branches were set up containing groceries, greengroceries, drapers, shoeshops, bakeries, butchers and furniture and hardware departments. The Co-op had its own factories supplying everything from beds to shoepolish, and paid its customer shareholders a dividend quarterly. The Co-op Bank was available for customers to save the 'divi' in. Most Co-op branches also had a hall library and reading room on the first floor above the shops. At Blaydon there was a separate hall on Shibdon Road, that was used for years as a cinema.

23. *The Co-operative Society jubilee 1908.* The popularity of the 'Co-op' amongst its members can be judged by the size of the crowds on this card. The photo shows the whole of Church Street, the tree to the right is in the churchyard. The building behind the tree was a billiard hall for many years. While the ladies display a wide range of millinary creations the men generally stick to caps and duts with only the occasional straw boater. The shop on the left is a shoeshop, kept by Mr. J. Windsor. He has displayed his wares by tying them to the edge of his sunshade. Mr. Windsor also used verse to drum up customers. In the 'Book of the Bazaar' published in 1903 to raise funds for a Church Hall, he wrote:

Don't throw away your old shoes
At weddings or elsewhere
Be grateful that they're easy
And send them for repair.

24. *Church Street, looking up to the south-west.* This is a very early postcard, it shows the shops and houses at the top of the street. The tower of St. Cuthberts can be seen over the roofs of the shops to the left. The trees at the top, along Garden Street, stand where the Plaza Cinema was to be build. The public house on the right was to be completely rebuilt as the Red Lion Hotel. When this card was produced pubs often brewed their own beer. One local brewer was 'Bewick Bros.' This firm produced ales and porter and aerated waters, two favourites being ginger beer and hop ale. These were delivered weekly by the brewers to the town terraces and the surrounding pit villages.

25. *Church Street looking north-west, about 1910.* Here we see the recently completed Red Lion. Its clean walls are in marked distinction to the older buildings opposite and the shops on the right. The buildings in industrial towns such as Blaydon quickly took on a layer of sooty grime, produced by the chimneys of the factories, houses and railway engines burning coal. This layer gave the town a gloomy look, often reflecting the grim conditions during recessions in trade such as the slump in 1930. Notice the two boys outside the Red Lion, looking towards the camera, still regarded as a curiosity outside the studio of the professional photographer. The long exposure necessary for this card has caused a moving person in front of the boys to take on a ghostlike transparency, with a solid shadow.

26. *St. Cuthberts Church, Blaydon about 1900.* The church stands at the junction of Church Street and Garden Street. It is built in early English style. Building commenced in 1844, when the nave and south porch were erected. The tower, aisle and chancel were added later and it gained the clock and bells in 1876. The first rector, Reverend Wm. Brown, built the church and the National School after the parish was established, from a division of the ancient Ryton parish. He died aged 59, following illness caused by a fall from the tower when it was being built. The name of the church and parish is 'St. Cuthberts, Stella'. This reflects the national rivalry of the time between the Anglican Church and the recently emancipated Roman-Catholic Church. Both claimed names that had associations with the pre-reformation church. 'Stella' had pedigree dating back to Norman times, it also had a more aristocratic image than the bustling and grimy working class reality that was Blaydon.

27. *An early photograph of Blaydon Church.* The dress of the subjects, and the lack of the tower on the church, make this the oldest image in this book. It shows the church as originally built, together with the first rector and his family. Reverend Brown is on the left, while the lady in the fine crinoline, fashionable at the time, is his cousin. Mrs. Brown is the lady squatting down in the dark dress, the other lady is another cousin while the maid was to become Mrs. Jane Somers. This photograph was supplied by Mr. J. Cunningham, for 'The Book of the Bazaar', published to help build the Church Hall in 1903. A copy of this book came to light recently, and we have been able to use the photograph here, thanks to the generosity of Mrs. Thompson of Runhead.

Catholic Church, Blaydon

28. *St. Joseph's Roman-Catholic Church, Blaydon.* This postcard shows the church shortly after it was built in 1898. St. Joseph's is one of five daughter churches of St. Mary & St. Thomas Aquinas of Stella. Unlike the mother church, built before catholic emancipation, and forbidden to face the highway, St. Joseph's could and does rival its Anglican neighbour across the road. Its imposing bulk with Welsh slate roof and old red sandstone walls, is ably reproduced here. The corrugated iron hall to its left is one of several in the district, all built around the turn of the century. The intricate ironwork railings seen here were to disappear into local foundries to help the war effort. The cobbles are no longer with us on the hill, as horse-drawn carts and traps have long ago been replaced by motor cars and lorries.

29. *Edward Street Blaydon 1918 armistice party.* The absence of men in the photograph is a reminder that the war effort in the Great War took most of the men away, leaving the ladies to run not just the homes but also the factories. The exodus of the men from the pits and factories starved factories of fuel and caused a shortage of shells at the front. This led the war cabinet during the 1939-45 War to keep the miners at the pit and actually conscript men into the mines. The grim faces of the adults in this photograph, after four years of total war, are in poignant contrast to the smiling faces of the bairns, dressed in their homemade costumes for the party.

Urban Council Offices, Blaydon

Valentines Series

30. *Blaydon U.D.C. Offices, about 1910.* This card shows the Council Offices, the Wesleyan Chapel and, on the left, the Co-operative Hall used as a picture house 'The Pavilion', as well as being the local office of 'The Foresters Friendly Society'. Blaydon U.D.C. was set up in 1894, to replace the local board constituted in 1891. The Council gained a certain notoriety in the 1930s, during the depression, when the level of acrimony and dissent expressed at meetings made the meetings so popular that public admission was by ticket only. It was about this time that a move was made to combine Blaydon and Ryton U.D.C's. This was resisted vigorously by both councils. The Wesleyan Chapel was built in 1893. It replaced the chapel built in 1856 in Wesley Place. The earliest meeting place for Blaydon's Methodists was in a house in Horsecrofts, built in 1737. The house was the home of William and Mary Howdon, it was demolished when Bridge Street was built in the early 1800's.

BLAYDON DENE.

31. *The dene Blaydon about 1910.* This card was taken by Mr. T. Friars, a Blaydon tradesman and one of the first private photographers in the district. It shows Blaydon Dene. The dene, together with the cemetery, formed the eastern boundary of the town streets that ran up from Shibdon Road. The wooded area of the dene was a popular walk for residents, especially after church or chapel on sundays. Today the dene is surrounded by housing, mostly built comparatively recently. Blaydon Main Colliery, sunk in 1853, on the site of the old Hazard pit near the bottom of Shibdon Bank, provided a major source of employment. It was one of the last pits to be sunk in the area without having its own 'pit rows'. Today the swimming pool occupies the old colliery site.

32. *Shibdon Road, Blaydon.* This card shows very clearly the rural nature of most of Blaydon and Winlaton. The card was produced by T. Friars, it shows a main road, between two very busy industrial centres, at Swalwell and Blaydon. The tree lined road, with its old stone wall, would not be out of place in a farming hamlet deep in the country. Only the telegraph poles, with their large weight of wires, give the evidence of its location between the two towns. One reason for the lack of road traffic was of course the railway lines which were particularly abundant in the area. Blaydon had passenger lines up the Derwent Valley and across to Scotswood as well as the Newcastle to Carlisle line to Gateshead and Hexham. Supplementing these was perhaps the densest concentration of mineral lines anywhere in the land, carrying coal to the Tyne and the main line.

33. *The Chemical Works, Blaydon Spike*. The parcel of land lying north of the main line and a few hundred yards east of the station, where the Tyne turns north for a short distance, is called 'Blaydon Spike'. This name is said to date back to 1856, when captured Russian guns were brought here after the Crimean War to be spiked. The community on the Spike lived in five terraces, worshipped in a Methodist chapel, and provided the bulk of the workers for the many factories here. The factories had their own railway sidings. This view shows the 'Manure and Alkali Co.' works. Horse and cow manure was processed here together with other farmyard slurry to produce potash, soda and phosphorus. In the 'laissez faire' commercial atmosphere of Victorian England, with few, if any, controls on pollution, the stench in and around the factory must have been horrendous. As late as the 1950s pleasure trip down the Tyne contained several odourous landmarks including this factory. Neighbouring factories included a Lampblack Works and a Bottle Works. The chimneys in the background belonged to the Firebrick Works.

34. *Upholstery Works, Blaydon.* This photograph was taken during the depression of 1930. Following the closure of many factories, and the laying off of thousands of workers by the pits and heavy engineering works, unemployment rocketed in Blaydon. Eventually government schemes were introduced to train men in new skills, and small units were set up to provide 'light industry'. This picture shows the interior of one such scheme, producing upholstered furniture. It is doubtful if its products could be afforded locally, as seven out of every ten men of Blaydon were condemned to idleness and penuary by the lack of real jobs. Only with the outbreak of the war in 1939 was there a revival in the local economy.

35. *Temporary housing, Blaydon Spike, about 1920.* At the end of the Great War, in an effort to build 'homes fit for heroes', plans were made to start building council housing. However, while these plans were being implemented, temporary housing was needed especially in towns like Blaydon, coping with an influx of workers, as industry boomed, and also with the return of demobilised troops all eager for a home of their own. One scheme used on the Blaydon Haughs, was to convert railway carriages into bungalows. This photograph shows the 'Pioneer', an 0-4-0 saddle tank locomotive built around 1870, and used around the Spike for shunting duties on the private lines, hauling one such 'bungalow'. Notice the new gas light, awaiting its lamp top, clock and mantle. Some of these 'temporary' houses were later extended by fitting a leanto on one side, one was in use for over fifty years before being replaced by a more conventional building.

36. *Scotswood Bridge.* This view of the bridge dates to about 1932, it is taken from the Blaydon Staithes near the mouth of the Derwent, looking upstream. It shows the bridge shortly after the chains had been replaced by steel hawsers. At the same time the bridge was widened by the addition of footpaths which ran outside the two towers supporting the cable and bridge. The bridge was opened on 16th April 1831, being one of the first chain suspension bridges built anywhere. Although it was designed for horse-drawn traffic it lasted well into the era of mass motoring. By 1921 it was already too narrow for modern traffic, but it was not replaced until 1967. Mr. Hall, the original engineer, could never have envisaged the traffic load it was to carry in its final half century of service. To the end there was a reminder of less hurried days in the notice on each tower ordering troops to break step when crossing the bridge.

37. *Bates Cottages about 1900.* These cottages, just off the Swalwell to Blaydon road, are on the site of a rural hamlet which predated by over a century the foundation of Swalwell as a centre for Crowley's ironworks. The hamlet developed around 'Bate's Mansion' a substantial house built about 1580. The railway line which crosses the road at this point was the Garesfield & Chopwell mineral line. This line was used to bring coal from the Priestman Collieries to the mouth of the Derwent for shipment down the Tyne or use at the brickworks there. The line also connected with the North Eastern Railway's Redheugh branch. About 3,000 tons of coal came down this line daily in the years before 1914.

Motor Bus Accident, Swalwell Bridge.

A.A. Fletcher
Printer & Publisher
Swalwell & Dunston.

38. *Motorbus accident, Turnpike Bridge, Swalwell.* This card printed in Fletchers Works just 200 yards down the road from the scene depicted, and on sale in the 1920's, aptly illustrates the popular interest in gruesome and macabre subjects following the Great War. Publishers all over Europe responded to and fed this appetite with books devoted to death in the trenches. The unfortunate char-à-banc crashed through the parapet of the old bridge with fatal consequences late one winter evening. The local doctor, called to the scene, had the corpse removed on the back of a lorry. This photograph was taken the following morning, notice the crowds on the Swalwell bank. The bridge, which crosses the Derwent, is on the boundary between Blaydon and Whickham U.D.C. It was built in 1760 by the Clavering family on the site of Selby's ford. The old ford was itself the scene of an earlier winter tragedy. During a blizzard in 1745 a horserider was swept to his death by the icy Derwent in spate.

39. *Axwell Villa about 1920.* The house stands in the estate of Axwell Hall called Axwell Park. It stands near the gate to the park on the Swalwell to Blaydon road. The lake it overlooks is artificial, constructed like the Serpentine in London, as an ornamental addition to the grounds of the park. The house windows at ground level are a variation of the local 'Durham Sash', having diamond lights instead of the familiar Georgian rectangles. Built originally as Dower House to the estate, it was renamed the 'Villa' when the estate was sold in 1920. The castellations around the roof proclaim its aristocratic connections. Axwell Hall was built and the park laid out by the Clavering family. James Clavering founded the family fortune by his marriage in the closing years of the 16th century to Grace Nicholson. This marriage brought him most of the Whickham & Gateshead Coal Industry. His grandson bought the estate after the restoration of Charles II and replaced the Whitehouse, which stood overlooking the Derwent, with Axwell Hall.

40. *Axwell Park Lake about 1910.* This card, photographed from outside the boundary wall to the Axwell estate, gives a good impression of the rural, even arcadian landscape, designed by the Claverings to enhance the outlook from the Hall. The successful landscaping of the estate completely disguises the fact that it was set amongst collieries, ironsworks, mineral wagonways and brickworks. This area was perhaps the most intensely industrialised corner of the whole kingdom, before what traditional historians call the 'Industrial Revolution' took place, and brought similar developments elsewhere.

41. *Axwell Lake, Footbridge about 1900.* This card taken inside the grounds, shows the footbridge that led across from the garden of the Dower House to the meadow that skirted the road to Winlaton Mill. The well-kept nature of the house at this time was due to the fact that the owners, the last baronet, then the Napier-Claverings actually used the house as the family home. This was in marked contrast to earlier baronets, the eighth, Thomas-John settled with his family in France in 1801 at St.-Germain-en-Laye. He was interned by Napoleon when hostilities resumed and remained a prisoner until 1814. His son James, having escaped, took a commission in the army and saw action under Wellington, sharing in the defeat of the armies of Napoleon in Spain and Portugal.

42. *Axwell Hall about 1920.* The Hall was designed and built by James Payne between 1758 and 1762. When it was built it was regarded as one of the premier mansions in the region, and a fitting home for the local member of Parliament for Durham County. Sir Thomas, the seventh baronet, was seen as a logical choice as M.P. for the coalmining county, given the fact that the miners themselves didn't have the vote. The mineowners of Durham were able until well into the 19th century, to exploit female and child labour, and accept horrendous pit accidents. Whole communities in the area were left fatherless due to the lack of rudimentary safety procedures, regarded by the owners as uneconomic. This situation was highlighted when Parliament, forced by public opinion, set up a committee to investigate child labour. The coal owning M.P.s and their allies 'packed' it but were unable in the face of the evidence to continue the exploitation they had practiced for centuries.

43. *Winlaton Mill.* The village of Winlaton Mill, taken from the North Eastern Railway branch to Consett. In the foreground is the 'Butterfly' footbridge over the river Derwent, in the background are the houses of the village. Winlaton Mill was one of the earliest Saxon settlements along the Derwent. The older, whitewashed houses with pantile roofs date to about 1700. Ambrose Crowley had them built as he set up a works to take advantage of the energy in the fast flowing river, establishing an iron mill. The possibility of being able to cross the river at this point is the reason why the village has had a continuous record of habitation for over a millenium. The road south up through Clockburn Woods leads eventually to Durham, so people who chose to cross the Tyne at the Ryton fords, to avoid law officers at Newcastle, could continue along the 'Corpse Route' to Winlaton and so down to the mill ford. This was the road taken by Cromwell's artillery in 1650 on route to Dunbar, avoiding the narrow bridge at Newcastle. The first mill here was the corn mill for the manor of Winlaton, the village also had a fulling mill 200 years before Crowley set up his works.

44. *Winlaton Mill, the village street.* This card shows the houses built for Crowley's workmen. Crowley set up his works as a mixture of 'factory' and 'cottage industry' units. He built a blade mill, to grind steel blades to a good edge, a steel furnace, a warehouse and a forge. However, much of the shaping and finishing of the iron and steel artifacts was done in blacksmith's forge units built facing into squares. At Winlaton Mill there were Old and New Squares. Crowley had a cradle to grave concern for his workers. He set up schools, a health service, and a pension scheme, these were funded from deductions off the workers pay. The little empire was governed by strict rules of conduct. Young men were forbidden to visit certain parts of Newcastle, or associate with known reprobates. The company built a balcony in the parish church, then at Ryton, and all workers were expected to attend divine worship, and encouraged to save in the savings bank run by the Rector.

45. *Winlaton Mill, village about 1920.* This is a photograph by Walter Tate intended for publication in the local press. It shows the old village being pulled down, and, in the background new housing built by the Blaydon U.D.C. By this time the iron works were long gone, and most of the men in the village were employed at one of the local collieries or the coke works a little way down the valley. Modern bridges over Tyne and Derwent had long ago left the village a backwater with few travellers, and no attempt was made to upgrade the Butterfly Bridge to carry a road or make up the old Clockburn lane road. When the modern village was designed it was decided to give the residents views across the countryside and up and down the valley. The houses were accordingly built with back gardens facing the Winlaton Road.

"The Big Tree", Nobbys Road End, Winlaton

46. *Nobby's Road end, Winlaton about 1910.* The road to the left leads to Winlaton Mill and Rowlands Gill, the road to the right to Normans Riding. This part of Winlaton to the south of the main village was a bleak and forbidding place, near here is Letch Wood, notorious for suicides by hanging from one of the beech trees. The most mysterious of these occurred in 1660, when a man hanged himself after reading the proclamation of the restoration of the monarchy. This stated that there would be no pardon for the regicides of Charles I. He was buried in the time honoured way, at the four lane ends with a stake through his heart. This road was part of the 'Corpse Road' from the mill to Ryton Churchyards to which all dead villagers were carried for burial. Most of the older buildings in the area near here have their own stories of ghostly happenings. The big tree acted as a landmark for travellers, hurrying along this lonely stretch. Today housing and street lighting have removed much of its eerie nocturnal atmosphere.

47. *St. Paul's Church, Winlaton about 1910.* The church was built in 1828 as a chapel of ease on the site of the village bullring. The parish of Winlaton was formed at the division of the ancient parish of Ryton in 1833. This was the first reorganisation of parish boundaries since Saxon times. Before St. Paul's was built the people had used a chapel, endowed by the Crowley Co. in 1705. This was done to prevent the workers being converted to Catholicism, or joining the 'Dissenters'. Both these sects were considered as revolutionaries by the management. The opening of St.Paul's ended the need for the villagers to travel to Ryton to take communion or bury their dead. The relationship between Church and villagers did not always run smoothly. The 'Brotherhood' of blacksmiths, which long survived the departure of Crowley's in 1815, brought them, as ratepayers, into conflict with the church vestry on several occasions. They successfully voted down a three half penny parish rate in 1858 and abolished it in 1868.

WINLATON SCHOOLS 4916 G.N.N/C.

48. *Winlaton board school about 1910.* When this card was produced the board school catered for about 500 pupils. Learning by rote and copybook repetition were backed by a strict discipline based on dunces cap and cane. One pupil of the time remembered seeing a boy being punished by being paraded through each class wearing sandwich boards proclaming his 'sin'; 'I have been caught smoking.' He was then caned. The school was erected in 1877 adding to the educational provision already provided by the 'National' school first opened in 1816. The National school taught the church catechism to all. The board school had no such religious bias, and was welcomed by non-conformist parents. By 1899 the old National school was in danger of losing its grant as the buildings were inadequate. A new church school was built and opened in 1902.

49. *Carousel, Winlaton Hoppings about 1910.* A collection of local schoolchildren pose on the 'Galloping Horses'. This annual fair, still going strong today, probably began as a trading fair in Saxon Northumbria. The Hoppings are held on the weekend following the 14th of May. Until comparatively recently the fairground stretched down the streets from Hood Square to Commercial Square. It is now confined to the 'windy fields' and the people of Hanover estate have a few late nights while the festivities are in full swing. The whole town took part in the fair. Friday night was opened with free rides on the amusements for the children. Saturday saw dances in the upper rooms of the public houses in the village, and on Sunday there was a church parade by the 'Volunteers' when locals and fairground folk crowded into St. Paul's. The 'Hoppings' even had its own song, written in 1830 by John Leonard, two lines of which reflect, prophetically, the staying power of the festival:

Sure Blaydon Races can't compare,
With Winlaton's famed Hopping, O

Church Street, Winlaton.

50. *Church Street, Winlaton about 1920.* The card shows the top of the township, with the tower of St. Paul's amongst the trees of the churchyard. The children are on their way to school, although most seem more interested in the camera. The cobbles on the left led to an iron foundry. The houses are a mixture of ages, the smaller ones in the terrace on the left probably date back to the early 18th century, being some of 'Crowley's Crew's' homes. The house with the smooth whitewashed rendering was destroyed by enemy bombs in the Second World War. It says much for the stonemasons of Winlaton, that the larger house survived the blast with only a few broken windows.

51. *Sandhill, Winlaton about 1900.* This card was in circulation from about 1900, it is a view east from the top of the hill up to Winlaton town from Low Town End. The large shop in the right foreground is a branch of Walter Willson. During the 1930s the smaller window belonged to a separate establishment, run by Mrs. Hall, who supplied knitting wool to the village. Sandhill is a placename that probably predates the village's association with the Crowley Co. It is a reminder of the 16th and 17th centuries when Winlaton was the main source of 'Sea coal' for London. One local coal baron, Sir William Blackett, lost £20,000 trying to sink a mine into the 'Sandhill' in the 1670s. The establishment of a school here by the Crowley Co. gained for Winlaton the nickname 'Knowledge Hill'.

52. *Sandhill from the north about 1910.* The large building on the right is the New Inn. This inn was used to billet troops during the Second World War. It was destroyed by fire towards the end of the war. Plenders drapery shop, left centre, was so successful that, by 1900, a branch was opened in Church Street Blaydon. The large roof with the pointed ventilator belongs to the Blaydon Co-op. It is one of the few buildings on the card that still stand today. The lack of much traffic in what was a busy town is a reminder that up to fifty years ago most people had to walk to get to local destinations. The village Bobby is also a reminder of a more localised existence than life as it is lived today.

Winlaton Vulcans, 1905-6.

WINNERS OF DURHAM 2ND SENIOR CUP AND CHAMPIONS OF JUNIOR INTER-COUNTY LEAGUE.

53. *Winlaton Vulcans Rugby Team, 1906.* This card, used by one of the team in 1909 to confirm a fixture, shows the whole team and the 'Management'. Sport cut across the otherwise rigid class barriers of Edwardian England, and so it was in Winlaton. This group included pitmen, blacksmiths, a factory owner, and the local doctor. Rugby football was and remains a popular game throughout the ancient parish of Ryton, and the three teams, Ryton, Blaydon and Winlaton Vulcans, were amongst the first to take up the sport in the North, this fact is signified by the plain Blue Ryton strip and the plain Red Blaydon strip. The Vulcan's history is not so unbroken as their parish neighbours, the club had to be restarted in the 1950s after a break of several years The photograph from which this card was produced was taken in a local studio, and displays the painted background of a rather opulant late Victorian interior. The curtains and wallpaper of William Morris' floral patterns are at odds with the image of the tough Vulcan team ready to pound their opponents into the ground!

Winlaton, The Village.

54. *Winlaton village, looking towards the Sandhill about 1900.* This card was taken by Francis Frith and shows the Sandhill before the building of the New Inn. The drapers shop is without railings, and the cottage behind and to the right can be clearly seen. Notice the striped pole erected in front of the barbers shop on the left, just next to the telegraph pole. The clarity of this card is due to the fact that Frith took 16 by 10 glass plates from which he printed his postcards. Older residents of the village will doubtless recall some of the shops seen here. Forty years ago they included Blands the cobblers, Armstrongs the drapers and the Papershop.

Front Street Winlaton

55. *Front Street Winlaton about 1900.* A busy street scene, but with little traffic about. The aptly named Smiths' Arms Hotel was one of many inns and public houses in Winlaton. It was a common saying in the district that 'every other house in Winlaton is a black-smiths or a pub'. The three storey building in the centre of the card was the old working mens club, while the building which appears to block the road gives the impression, noted by Bourne in 1895, that little planning had gone into the development of Winlaton. In fact he was wrong! The Crowley Company planned its building in 'squares', where the smiths lived and worked. They were not allowed to leave their square during working hours without permission from the square monitor. It was the surviving buildings from the Crowley period, that gave sharp angles to the road bends and created an impression of chaotic planning.

56. *Front Street, Winlaton.* Another view of Front Street, taken from an angle which shows that the road continues past the end building. This card shows a few changes to the previous picture, Rowell & Son has become Mc. Fail & Co. The smaller building on the left was the home of the Robinsons, father and son were both employed as rent collectors by the private landlords of the village. The pantile roofed building behind the cottage was a blacksmith's shop. Long shadows rather obscure the right of the photograph, causing the straw sailor's hat and the ladies' aprons to stand out. This is in marked contrast to the brightness of the building on the far left, where detail has been lost because of the light. Winlaton at this time had an interesting mixture of paved and cobbled footpaths, as on the right, and unpaved but curbed footpaths as on the left. Look out for the same mixture on other cards.

57. *Winlaton White Star sword dancers, 1924.* This is the team that won national fame. They won the North of England Musical Tournament Cup outright by taking it in 1922, 1923 and 1924, and appeared in the Albert Hall in 1927. The names of the dancers were Chris. Boyd (piper), Geo. Gilfillin, R. Bilclough, W. Prudhoe, Jos. Gardner, John Renwick and Geo. Renwick. Their aggregate age was 475 years. The sword dance dates back to pagan times, and is associated with Odin, the God of the smiths, the magical properties attributed to iron and the men who worked it. When William Gilbert, physician to Elizabeth I, accurately described the laws of magnetism, he did so in term of 'Iron's magical attractive forces'. In medieval science any action at a distance, except gravity, was described as 'magic'. The swords in the picture were over 100 years old when they were replaced in 1955. The group had five dancers and two clowns (the 'Tommy' and the 'Nancy') and a piper. As well as appearances at music festivals, the group, who were most secretive about the dance, often appeared in the inns of Winlaton, and made a perambulation of the village at Christmas time. While the group danced, the 'Nancy' collected beer money for them.

58. *Winlaton Village looking north.* This is another card by Francis Frith, taken in 1900. Mr. Frith spent fifty years, from 1880 to 1930, travelling around England and producing postcards. In that time he took over 40,000 glass plate photographs. The best were then used to print up as postcards. Once again Winlaton's preponderance of public houses is in evidence, the Highlander on the right, the Queens Head on the left. The small shop down the road from the Queens Head was the village Post Office. The road going off to the left led past the Congregational Church, just in view behind the Highlander, past the oldest part of the village 'Back Street', then on past the 'Rex' Cinema and the Wesleyan Church on Lichfield Lane to the top of Blaydon Bank about 3/4 of a mile away.

59. *Thomas Prudhoe, chainmaker, in 1910.* The gentleman in the photograph was 92 when he posed for this study nearly eighty years ago. He served his apprenticeship with men who were part of 'Crowley's Crew' and the skills he was taught by them were those they had used to fashion the anchor chains of Nelson's Fleet. The superiority of their workmanship over their continental rivals was demonstrated in the storm after the Battle of Trafalgar. Not a single Royal Navy ship lost its anchors, but all 17 French and Spanish prizes were lost, blown onto the rocks of the Brittany Coast or floundering, when their anchor chains snapped.

60. *The Congregational Church*. This card shows the church shortly after it was built in 1905. Prior to this the congregation had worshipped in a chapel built in 1829. This stood a little way back in Joblings Garth, behind the church shown here. The church site had been used for chapels in previous centuries. A Catholic chapel dedicated to St. Anne served the pre-reformation village. It was burned down in 1569. Crowley's manager erected a chapel for the 'crew' to use here in 1705. The minister at the time the church was built was the Reverend Albert B. Tebb. He was instrumental in not only building the chapel, but also active on the school board and the Blaydon U.D.C. The boy in the foreground is holding an iron hoop, called a gird, and an iron hook. The gird was set in motion and controlled using the hook. Toys like this were produced in the smithies of the town from scraps of spare iron.

61. *A Winlaton Blacksmith outside his smithy*. This smithy stood on Church Street. After the Crowley Company ceased operations in Winlaton in 1815, the out of work blacksmiths were forced to set up on their own account. In order to continue to receive the welfare benefits they had enjoyed under Crowley, they also started a 'Blacksmiths' Friendly Society' of which Jos. Cowen Sn. was a founder member. The village economy improved as coal demand grew with the coming of the steam locomotive and stationary steam engines replaced water mills as the main source of power in factories. So, while the great days of 'Crowley's Crew' were gone for ever, the village smithies were kept busy manufacturing nails, hinges and chains. The last chain made in Winlaton was forged in 1966, thus ending a quarter of a millenium of chain making. The Crowley Co. not only made chains, they also forged the gates of Buckingham Palace in a smithy in Church Street.

62. *Front Street Winlaton about 1910.* The road leads to Commercial Square. On the right of the photograph are buildings which include an iron foundry and a chain maker, as well as the inevitable pub. Notice the man with the bicycle walking up the hill. One of the disadvantages of Winlaton for the cyclist was the number of hills that had to be climbed on the roads back from Blaydon, Ryton or Winlaton Mill. The hills from Winlaton down to Blaydon, Shibdon Bank and Blaydon Bank, were particularly long and steep. On one occasion in the 1920s there was a serious char-à-banc accident on Blaydon Bank with fatal consequences, when the brakes failed. The Congregational Chapel stood at the top of the two long inclines that ran down towards the two banks to Blaydon. The old coal owners used these hills to advantage, sending the coal in carts down 'gravity inclines' on early wooden railways. The horses needed to pull the empty carts back up rode down on the specially designed backs of the carts.

63. *George V Coronation Celebrations, Winlaton 1911.* The procession, in fancy dress, is making its way past Commercial Square. Once again the remains of Crowley's architecture give the place an unplanned appearance. In front of the Commercial Hotel is the site of Crowley's factory farm. This was called Broomly Close Farm. Behind the hotel are recently built streets running along to Clara Street. The procession includes the town band, also in costume. Commercial Square was one of three squares established by the Crowley Co. The sites of the other two are at Hood Square, just south of Sandhill, and Hanover Square, near the Low Town End, The Crowley Co. encouraged loyalty amongst the 'crew', the names of the squares reflect this. Loyalty to the commercial system, the ruling dynasty and the navy (Admiral Hood was Snr. Admiral at the time) that gave the factory orders for chains. The Crew's discipline and loyalty to itself took on another face when the Crowley Co. abandoned them. The blacksmiths became supporters of radical politics and the Chartist movement. This support included the manufacture of weapons, pikes and cra feet (used to unseat cavalry) after the Peterloo massacre.

64. *George Armstrong's smithy Winlaton.* This shows a typical Blacksmith's shop in the village. The owner, with his family, stands at the door. The smithies at Winlaton each kept to their own specialities, avoiding open competition with each other. It is still possible to find examples of their work around the area. For example the gates of the home of the Hirst family, who ran a bus service until the 1950s, are secured on hinges made by the great grandfather of the present occupant. Each hinge bears the legend: 'Hirsts, Blacksmiths, Winlaton.' Other smithies made nails, wrought iron work, locks, bolts and, of course, chains. Today the craft is remembered in a restored smith's shop, set out with the tools of the trade and historic notes for the visitor, relating Winlaton's long association with Vulcan's trade.

65. *Winlaton, Hoppings Parade, about 1920.* The Hoppings holiday weekend always included a church parade on Hoppings Sunday morning. This card shows the parade as it passes by the footpath to the 'windy Fields, heading up the hill from the Low Town End to the church. Once again the cloth cap is much in evidence, with only an occasional 'dut'. The ladies section in the parade, just behind the 'Volunteers' are St. Johns Ambulance Brigade Nurses. The Brigade organised the parade at the time that this card was produced. The tradition leaders of the parade were the Winlaton Brass Band, which was one of the oldest in the country, dating back to 1800. Early engagements for the band involved accompanying 'Crowley's Crew', and later, playing at Chartist Rallies in the town.

66. *View of Blaydon from Winlaton.* A postcard showing the bend in the River Tyne around Blaydon Spike and the streets which run up Shibdon road towards Winlaton. The houses on the right run down Blaydon Bank. At this time Blaydon, Winlaton and Bleach Green were clearly separated communities with considerable areas of open farmland between them. In marked contrast was Blaydon Burn, today a stream being actively developed as a country park. The burn was then a corridor of industry. It had mines at the village and a water wheel to drive a generator used to provide electricity to the Surtees family mansion which overlooked the village from the south. In addition there were a tar works and several mills downstream. The mills had been used in former days for iron working, flint grinding cotton and fulling as well as grinding corn. Finally there stood a brickworks where the burn met the Tyne at Blaydon. Blaydon Burn has been described by industrial archeologists as 'The Coalbrookdale of the North'.

67. *Greenwell Farm, Blaydon Burn.* A photograph of the farmyard at Robinson's farm. The farm fields are today almost all covered with houses built since 1945. This housing effectively joins the two townships of Blaydon and Winlaton into a single urban area. The card is a reminder of the large part played by the cart horse in pre-war transportation, as well as providing most of the power around the farm. The pit pony played a similar role underground. The Robinson family ran a butchery business in Blaydon town as well as the farm.

68. *Blaydon Burn Village looking north-west about 1900.* The village had two drift mines, the 'Mary' and the 'Bessie'. These worked east and west of the village. The small building in the right foreground, on a siding of the mineral railway which continued (right) down the burn, housed the 0-4-0 saddle tank locomotive, build by Hawthornes, for the Coal Co. The railway continued (left) for a short distance over hoppers, through which coal could be discharged into horse-drawn wagons for local delivery. The large number of chimneys in the background belonged to the 'brickflats'. These were brick ovens, and could be found at most local collieries. They produced bricks for local use by the coal Co. The bricks carried the name of the company or the colliery, and were a by-product of the mines in which was found firebrick clay in the strata between the coal seams. 'Useless' shale and clay were heaped in a hill to the north-east of the village. In the 1960s the whole pitheap was removed and sold for hardcore to the road building industry.

69. *Blaydon Burn Village, about 1920.* This card shows further development of the mines. In the foreground are the corrugated iron screening sheds. The large chimney belonged to the colliery boilerhouse. One problem with the location of the Colliery Yard at Blaydon Burn was that it was well 'Down the hill' from the local market for coal at Winlaton. To facilitate the transport of coal to Winlaton an aerial wagonway known locally as the 'Flight' was constructed from the colliery to the four lane ends. The large buckets on the wire were filled at the screens and carried up to the 'Flight', where they automatically discharged their load in a hopper. The colliery rows built down from North Street were so steep that they made coal delivery very hazardous for the horse-drawn coalcarts. This often meant that the coal was left at the top of the street, and had to be manhandled in buckets to the house.

70. *The Bessie drift about 1920*. This photograph taken in the 1920s, shows the mineral line which went down the Burn. Notice the left branch which goes under the winding house and the right branch disappearing into the drift. Standard gauge rails were rarely used, as here underground. Most railways inside the pit were narrow gauge, using small iron wagons, called tubs. The tubs were pulled around underground by pit ponies, and were small enough to be manhandled individually when full. Standard gauge trucks were sent by hawser into the drift to an underground hopper where they were filled from the tubs and then hauled out again. A locomotive was used for moving the trucks down the line to Blaydon, and one of them, a saddletank, can be seen in the shadows under the winding house.

71. *Blaydon Burn looking south-east.* This card shows the village from the road to Greenside, it dates from about 1920. In the background to the left of the woodland can be seen Blaydon Burn House. In the foreground is the pit yard and the buildings containing the workshops of the pit and houses for colliery overmen. In the yard is the pit prop stockpile. The props were used to support the roof in the underground workings. Older miners could often tell, by listening to the creaking of the props, when the roof was about to fall in. This fact is immortalised in a mining song in which an older miner cautions his eager son: 'Many a marras missing lad, Because he wouldn't listen lad.' Miners worked in pairs and were paid as a pair. One man in such a pair was always referred to as the other's 'marra'.

72. *Provision delivery 1910.* This postcard is one taken by Mr. Friar's camera, and shows him delivering to one of the cottages along Sandy Bank Road. The building to the left of the cottage is a combined coal house and earth closet. The small door at the bottom of the building was used to remove the night soil. This toilet arrangement was standard in pit villages around the area. For sanitary reasons the 'Netty', as it was called, was built away from the house. This usually meant at the bottom of the yard, backing onto the road, so the nightsoil could be removed, and the coalhouse filled, from the road. Occasionally the 'Netty' was built across the road. When this happened unsuspecting travellers on the road at night could be startled by the appearance of a nightshirted figure darting out of the Netty. The lady of the house wears a pinafore and cloth cap, a common form of working dress in the area.

73. *The Blaydon Burn flint mill about 1900.* The Blaydon Burn was industrialised for centuries before the 'Industrial Revolution'. There was shipbuilding at its mouth into the Tyne until the 1800s, and the rushing waters of the burn were dammed and mill races built to provide power. This old building, in the valley of the burn, was used as a flint mill. The use of water power for fulling, grinding flints and, later, iron working, was developed from flour milling both here and at Winlaton Mill. In earlier days, when the land in the Ryton parish belonged to the Bishop, building mills was kept as his monopoly. Only after the Reformation extra mills were built, and alternative uses found for the power they produced. This, together with the development of coal mining, industrialised this area centuries before most of the rest of Britain.

74. *Ottovale coke works, Blaydon Burn 1930s.* This card, from the end of our period, shows the plant which stood on the South bank of the Burn halfway between the village and Blaydon. The ovens were built between the wars by German engineers, and were a target for the Luftwaffe during the Second World War. Incendary bombs were dropped in one raid, and while the Blaydon auxiliary firemen were putting out the blaze, one fireman was killed by machinegun fire from a German plane. The same raid blew the glass roof of the railway station and scattered a newly delivered load of manure in an allotment near Clara Street Winlaton, across half the town. A subsequent broadcast by Lord Haw-haw boasted about the raid and warned the people of Barlow, near Winlaton, that they would be next. This promise was never fulfilled! The fumes from the coke ovens were considered to have medicinal properties, and local children with bronchial problems were taken 'a walk around the ovens', to relieve their congested lungs.

75. *Blaydon Burn Brickworks about 1900.* A view across the works from the mineral line which brought coal and fireclay from the mines. The two workmen on top of the ovens are enjoying their 'Bate', or mid-day snack. The tops of the ovens, as they were cooling after a brick-baking, would provide a comfortable seat during cold winter weather. The housing in the background gives an impression of how this part of Blaydon looked before the demolition of most of Bridge Street when the new road bridge was built across the burn. Some of the houses to the right of the picture still stand, much modernised and without the wooden privies, on what remains of Horse Crofts.

76. *Blaydon Burn brickworks looking towards Image Hill about 1900.* This card shows the lower ranks of the brick works. In the right background is the summerhouse of Stella Hall, which stands on top of Summerhill. The house originally had a domed roof and was used as a school in the early years of the 19th century. Behind the row of railway wagons can be seen the houses which line the old lead road up Summer Hill Bank. The house, partially obscured between the tree and the chimneys of the ovens, is Stella House, the one time home of the Silvertop family. Summerhill was given the name 'Image Hill' in the later 19th century, as Joseph Cowens erected several statues to prominent continental reformers, the most famous of these was Garabaldi. The ovens were used to produce bricks containing messages to patriots and nationalists to encourage their struggles for freedom against the autocracies of the Prussian, Russian and Austro-Hungarian Empires.

This ends 'Blaydon in old picture postcards'. For an account of the rest of the old parish of Ryton, see 'Ryton in old picture postcards', also by N.G. Rippeth.